Instant Insights on...

Unconventional Methods for Writing a Best Selling Book

PARVIZ FIROUZGAR

Crescendo
PUBLISHING

Instant Insights on ...
Unconventional Methods for Writing a Best Selling
Book
By Parviz Firouzgar

Copyright © 2017 by Parviz Firouzgar

Crescendo Publishing, LLC
300 Carlsbad Village Drive
Ste. 108A, #443
Carlsbad, California 92008-2999

www.CrescendoPublishing.com
GetPublished@CrescendoPublishing.com
1-877-575-8814

ISBN: 978-1-944177-71-3 (P)
ISBN: 978-1-944177-72-0 (E)

Printed in the United States of America
Cover design by Melody Hunter

10 9 8 7 6 5 4 3 2 1

What You'll Learn in This Book

Many people have thought about writing a book as they intuitively know they have a story to share that could benefit others. However, most people don't know how to go about the process. When searching for information on how to write a book, most find structured methods that are meant to apply to all people, but this does not necessarily work as we all have different styles, likes and dislikes, and ways of going about completing a project. For this reason we should find what works best for us so that we can enjoy the process, which will make the final product better as it then becomes a labor of love versus a chore. That is what this book will teach you: how to find your unique style so that you can have an infinitely greater chance to create the best book you are capable of writing.

In this book, you'll get **Instant Insights** on ...

- Finding the book that is inside you

- Learning several methods of planning and writing, in an effort to find the one that suits your unique style

- Teaching yourself to be a better writer

- Overcoming writer's block, something every author occasionally experiences

- The new world of marketing and how to turn your book into a substantial source of income

- The importance of enjoying the process and learning how writing can become a joyful experience for you unlike any other

A Gift from the Author

A free bonus chapter on the topic of creating success is available for you to download at any time.

You can get access to the complimentary materials on the author's website here:

www.successlibrary.com

Dedication

This book is dedicated to all of those brave first-time authors who overcame their fears and just went ahead and did it anyway.

There is a best seller inside each of us, including YOU!

Table of Contents

Introduction

I am occasionally asked to speak at book-writing conferences because I am told that I give good advice to first-time authors. This caused me to think more deeply about the art and practice of writing, an activity I enjoy beyond words (no pun intended).

The main question I pondered was whether there is a formula to good writing that anyone can or should follow. My opinion is that there should not be, although most books written to teach you how to write try to box you into some sort of formula. I believe that everyone has different habits, different styles, and different levels of enjoyment they receive from writing. Therefore I believe that everyone should follow what works for them, and not some rigid formula.

What I will strive to accomplish with this collection of tips and lessons is to help you find your particular style, the one that you should cultivate and the one that will make you an effective writer, hopefully even a best-selling author. Once you discover your style, your personality should shine through your words.

The only genre where I have found a specific formula that authors must follow is in writing romance novels, not because they must all be similar but because certain publishers require them for their own commercial reasons. If you read romance novels, you will notice a pattern that repeats itself from book to book. This is the pattern that publishers look for when considering your novel for publishing, especially if you want to be published by Harlequin.

Most other writing is not so rigid. Every writer has, and should have, their own style, tone, and method for moving through the process. This includes overcoming issues that sometimes hold authors back, such as writer's block. Your style does not necessarily have to be original. What's important is that it is one you enjoy and one that works for you to help you produce the best you are capable of producing.

When people who know me personally read my books, they often tell me that they can hear my voice as they read. I write similar to how I speak, and I write best when I write in a conversational tone. I want to help you find whatever tone works best for you also. That's what this book is about.

There will also be some lessons on universally valuable skills that will help you (regardless of what you write about), skills that every writer should cultivate. These skills help improve your final product regardless of what genre your book may fall into. But again, much of the process is very personal and you have to find what works best for you in those areas rather than following some rigid rules that don't jive with your likes, dislikes, and personality.

I taught myself to write, which means that when I started out, my writing was not so great. I listened to some critiques and then developed a few methods I used to continually improve my writing until I was at a level sufficient to publish a book. I will share those techniques with you.

Although I have written many books, I cannot express enough how important it is to have an editor to correct or improve spelling, punctuation, sentence structure, and grammar issues. Even the best writers continue to use and rely on editors throughout their careers. Very few will ever master the game to the point where an editor becomes superfluous.

Good editors also provide feedback on content when there is something inadvertently inappropriate or factually questionable. So don't think that the goal is perfection. It is not. The goal is to find the right style that works for you, to learn to love the experience of writing, to learn some skills valuable to all authors regardless of genre, and, of course, to make your writing good enough to become commercially successful.

The lessons in this book will reference the habits and style that I follow, but they will often serve merely as examples. Your style may be different. Nonetheless, these lessons will hopefully still serve their primary purpose: for you to find your own style and methods for moving through every phase of writing your book. The result will be that you'll learn to enjoy the process, something that will undoubtedly make you a much better writer than if writing did not become a labor of love for you.

This manual is not intended to be an all-encompassing, A-to-Z set of instructions that covers all aspects of the writing process. Instead, I'm offering a group of lessons that have helped me become a better writer and that will hopefully help you become a good writer too. Most of these I discovered myself, and that is typically what qualifies the lesson to be included here. Standard topics like grammar lessons or how to find a publisher can be found in an endless number of books elsewhere and won't be included here.

In summary, what I am trying to convey to you is that this is not a manual that includes everything you need to know about writing a book. It is a manual that contains some original and possibly unconventional tips, ideas, and lessons that should be useful to you, from a perspective you may not find elsewhere.

Your Instant Insights...

- Everyone has different habits, different styles, and different levels of enjoyment they receive from writing. Therefore, there should be no single formula for writing a book.

- This book is designed to help you find your particular style, tone, and method for going through the process of writing a book, one that suits you and that you enjoy.

- You can teach yourself to write well. The tips, ideas, and lessons in this book will show you how.

What should you write about?

*"The meaning of life is to find your gift.
The purpose of life is to give it away."*

– William Shakespeare

Everyone has a book in them just waiting to be put on paper. We all have an expertise others can learn from. We have also all had experiences that taught us unique lessons that can benefit those who read about them.

Everyone's life is a unique laboratory, unlike anyone else's. What is it about your life, your knowledge, and your experiences that the world wants — or even needs — to hear? What are you most passionate about? This is important, as it is often the area where your greatest expertise can be found. Because it is your passion, it will also likely be the area you'll most enjoy writing about, which will make your writing better as you let your passion shine through your words.

For me, my greatest passion and expertise lie in creating and teaching. In fact, it is who I am. Creating and teaching define me. Writing a book is an act of creation and what I write about teaches valuable skills to my readers. What is it that defines you? Ask yourself, "Who am I?" and write down the first words that come to mind.

Most of my books have been about entrepreneurship. That is, I teach you how to escape a nine-to-five lifestyle, follow your life's passion and purpose, AND become hugely successful in the process — without chance of failure. My entire adult life has been a laboratory for precisely these lessons, and they are the ones I most enjoy writing about. The reason is simple: I learned through experience how to make every entrepreneurial venture I pursue successful. You can do the same.

The techniques I have learned — often through trial and error, mistakes and failures, successes and observation of others — have taught me a set of skills that can make success a predetermined certainty. I love sharing those skills and lessons because I love seeing others succeed. I especially love the feeling of fulfillment I get when my teachings contribute to those successes.

If you think you haven't learned certain life lessons or that you have no valuable knowledge to share, you are probably wrong. Almost everyone has.

You just have to figure out what unique laboratory your life has been a vessel for. Here's an example.

Recently I talked to an acquaintance who has had the unfortunate experience of being homeless several times throughout his life. He described for me some of the techniques he learned for surviving on the streets and told me about the many government programs available to help those who find themselves in similar unfortunate circumstances. Most of these programs are little known to the homeless, and his sincere desire was to help other homeless people discover them to make life a little easier for them. I immediately resonated with his vision and realized that even a homeless person knows things that can substantially help others. The obvious conclusion is that we all have skills and knowledge that could fill a book that would be infinitely valuable to others.

Allow me to inspire you. You have a unique and valuable gift that your life experience has given you. The world wants you to share it, even if you don't yet know what that gift is.

Your Instant Insights...

- Everyone has a book inside them. It comes from your experiences and life lessons. Others can benefit from reading about them in a book that you write.

- What you're most passionate about is often where your greatest expertise can be found. This may often be your best topic for a book.

- Even a homeless person has learned lessons that can benefit others.

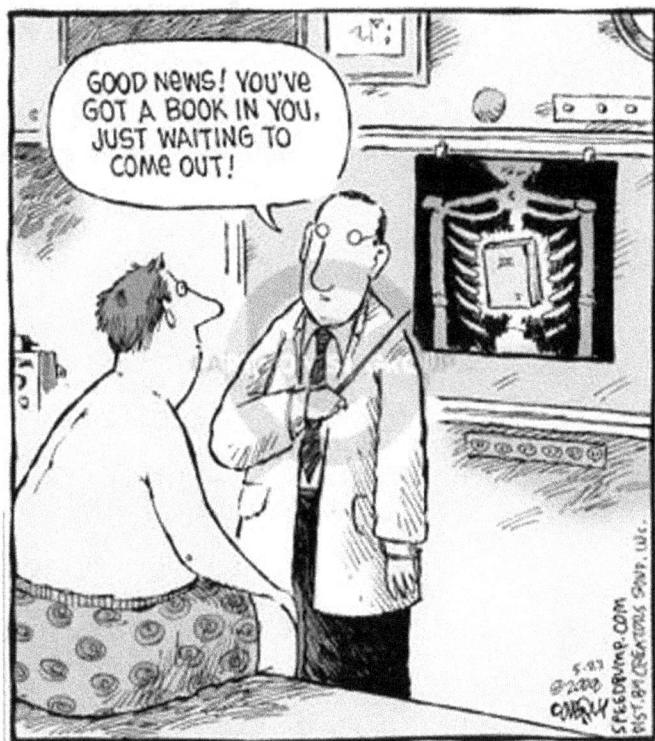

How to plan the writing of your book

This is where you will immediately see how everyone is different, and where you will come to understand that everyone should find the way to structure and go about writing their book in a way that works best for them. This is important because if you follow some formula where the methodology isn't suited to your personality, you will not enjoy the process and will likely give up on completing your book. It should be a labor of love, not a chore.

There are two main ways to go about writing your book. The first is to sit down and just start writing. You may already have the entire story in your head, or you may take it to the extreme by sitting down and starting to write without knowing exactly where your story or information is headed. I have done this. In fact, I once wrote a romance novel where I sat down and just started writing without any clue of where the story would lead. Although I never attempted to publish the book, it ended up being a good story (according to those who read my manuscript).

The other way is to create an outline first. The easiest way to do that is to think of the chapter headings in an order that makes sense for your book. Once you've designed your table of contents, you start filling in the text for one chapter after another. This is a very structured approach that is hard to argue with. You can even get more detailed in your planning by creating a list of subheadings under each chapter title.

Again, whatever method you choose, whether you just start writing, create an outline first, or use some sort of hybrid between the two, it should feel right to you. However, this doesn't mean that once you choose one method, you will always stick to it. I have written books using an outline I created first, others using a partial outline, and others still where I just started writing without any specific path or even an ending in mind. It can vary from book to book. I do whatever I feel like and what feels right to me, and like I said, it may change from book to book. You can approach your writing in similar fashion.

A hybrid method — probably the method I use the most — that works well for me is making a list of ideas that come to mind that I'd like to include in a book. They can be chapter headings or just thoughts of something I'd like to include. They are in no particular order and can be sorted into a logical order later. I also create lists of famous quotes that are on topic with my planned book.

You can also use your list to decide whether you should move forward in creating a final product. Once you have enough bullet points so that you can see the value of putting them all together into a book, you'll know it is time to move forward. If you cannot think of enough ideas to fill a book, you can set that list aside and see if more ideas come to you later. This process can take just a few days or a few years. You'll know when you have enough and when, or if, you should start writing.

I also like this hybrid method because I can have several lists for several books that I'm interested in writing. It provides a little structure, but most importantly, it allows me to record ideas so that I don't forget them, especially if it's a book I may not start writing for some time. If I am adding notes to the lists for several different book ideas, I will know exactly which one to start first, depending on which list gets completed the soonest or which book idea inspires me the most.

Your Instant Insights...

- There are three main methods for planning the writing of your book. The first is without structure where you just start writing. You don't even need to have a path or ending in mind.

- The second is to create an outline of chapter topics first. This is the most structured approach and can be further refined with subheadings underneath each chapter title.

- The third is a hybrid method where you make a series of notes of ideas to write about and then use those in whatever order feels right. You write them down in list format so that you don't forget them, but not in any specific order. They can even include famous quotes you want to use in your text.

Teaching yourself to write well

*"We are all apprentices in a craft where
no one ever becomes a master."*

— Ernest Hemingway

When I started to write, I did not write well. Several severe criticisms gave me the reality shock that I needed to figure out that I had to improve my writing skills. I started writing because I enjoyed writing, but I also wanted other people to read what I wrote and be impressed by it. When I started out, I simply wasn't yet ready for prime time, so I tried a few methods of teaching myself how to better my skills. They worked, and I believe they can work for you too.

This chapter will also include some valuable tips on writing styles that you can incorporate immediately to make your writing more commercially viable.

The first thing I did was to read popular books with a new set of eyes. As I read, I paid attention to sentence structure, sentence length, vocabulary, and style. In essence, I analyzed other authors' styles as I read their books. It is not hard to do. It's just a matter of paying attention not just to the meaning of the words you read but also to how the words are delivered. In fact, you can start doing this right now, reading this book.

The first thing I discovered about my writing was that my sentences were way too long. This got me to start reading what I wrote with different eyes. I started rereading my work over and over again, observing everything from a third-party perspective. It was almost like creating another person, detached from myself, who read my writing simultaneously with me, as I read it. That third party had a critical eye and looked for areas that did not flow smoothly or anything else of subpar quality.

Of course, I first had to learn what quality writing was, the type that was commercially viable. I discovered some of these elements by analyzing the works of one of my favorite fiction authors, Michael Crichton. He wrote *The Andromeda Strain*, *Jurassic Park*, *Rising Sun*, *Timeline*, *The Great Train Robbery*, and many more. What I noticed was how effortless it was to get through any of his books and how quickly I would finish them. Obviously, they were great stories, but there are lots of great stories out there, many of which are nowhere near as easy to read.

In analyzing Crichton's style, I noticed two things. The first was that his chapters were always short. This discovery was quite profound, as most of us habitually check ahead to see the length of the next chapter to determine whether we want to start on it now or later. If the next chapter is twenty-five pages long, we will typically put the book aside for another day. But if the chapter is only four or five pages long, we often say to ourselves, "I've got time for that." And then we do the same with the next chapter and the next. Ultimately this leads to reading the entire book in just a couple sittings. The lesson for me was obvious: Unless absolutely warranted, I shy away from writing long chapters. It's better to have lots of short ones.

Then I noticed something else. Michael Crichton wrote using seventh-grade language. He never tried to impress with grandiose vocabulary that most people don't understand unless they are constantly checking a dictionary at their side. In today's society, where most people's vocabulary and reading skills have unfortunately been dumbed down, coupled with their ever-shortening attention spans (hence the short chapters), it makes sense to tailor your writing style to your audience's reading skills and habits. It is the current *zeitgeist*, a German word that means sign of the times.

Another trend that has gained momentum is to write similarly to how we speak, in a very conversational tone. This has definitely benefitted me as people who know me always tell me that they can hear my voice when they read my books.

Short chapters, seventh-grade language and vocabulary, and a conversational tone are all styles I would urge you to consider incorporating into your writing. It will make your book infinitely more readable and enjoyable, even to a sophisticated audience. It simply doesn't benefit you when you try to impress your readers with your knowledge of words that few people understand. If you don't know what I mean, then open a book by Umberto Eco (*The Name of the Rose*, *Foucault's Pendulum*) and read a few paragraphs. Then read Michael Crichton or James Patterson. You'll get my point immediately.

Finally, another thing that I do, which has become very important to the quality of my writing, is that I review what I write many times. That is, once completed, I reread every chapter over and over again. Each time I make little corrections and improvements that eventually make my chapters better and better, fine-tuning them with every review. I would urge you to do the same.

Your Instant Insights...

- Learn to write by paying close attention to how other authors write. Do this while reading their books.

- It is often best to write using seventh-grade language and short chapters. This makes it easier for your readers to keep reading. Complicated language and long chapters cause readers to repeatedly postpone reading for another day. You can also write in a conversational tone.

- Reread what you write many times and make little corrections and improvements with each review. (I will touch on this subject further in a later chapter.)

Writer's block!

If there's one thing that every writer eventually experiences, it's writer's block — sitting there for hours, not knowing what to write next. It is the proverbial staring at a blank page with a blank mind. I've experienced it, and you'll experience it also.

There is no set way for overcoming writer's block, only different methods you can try to see what works best for you. I use two different methods, and both of them work very well for me.

All of us have used the first method before, but typically we never knew we were using it and even if we did, we didn't know what made it work. Consider this: Have you ever forgotten someone's name and thought about it really, really hard, but it still wouldn't come to you? You probably did this almost to the point of exhaustion until you just gave up and forgot about it. And then the strangest and most wonderful thing happened.

You woke up in the middle of the night with the name in your mind. What just happened?

The truth is that you just employed a very valid method for remembering something you have forgotten, for solving a problem, or for achieving a goal. You just didn't know you were doing it and certainly didn't know — and probably still don't know — what made it work. Well, here's the why and how of it so that you can consciously use this method to remember, solve problems, and even achieve almost any goal you can conceive. And, of course, you can also use it to overcome writer's block.

This method involves the mobilization of your subconscious mind. Our conscious mind is only about 10 percent of our total brainpower. The remaining 90 percent is our subconscious mind. It is like an iceberg where 90 percent of the volume and mass is unseen under the surface of the water. Only about 10 percent is visible. This tells us how much more powerful our subconscious abilities are.

So, here's what happened, and this will also explain how you can make it work for you whenever you want to tap into this technique in a preplanned way, such as overcoming writer's block.

From our previous example, when you forgot the name and consciously did everything you could to try to remember it but couldn't, you were actually in the beginning stages of getting your subconscious mind involved in solving your dilemma for you. That is, your conscious 10 percent was giving signals to your subconscious 90 percent to wake up and get involved. Then, and this is key, you gave up and forgot about the whole thing. This action mobilized your subconscious to take over. When it eventually comes up with the solution, it will pop into your mind, sometimes in the middle of the night. Unbeknownst to you, your subconscious has been working on your behalf the entire time.

So, whether it is remembering a name, solving a problem, coming up with a path that will lead you to a goal where previously you couldn't see a path, or overcoming writer's block, this is what you do. You consciously try to solve the issue. You think about it as hard as you can, almost to the point of exhaustion. Sometimes this is sufficient to come up with the answer you seek, but often it is not. If not, then after your period of intense concentration, you let go completely. You literally forget about the issue, knowing that you have just activated your subconscious abilities to go to work for you. At some point over the next couple days, the answer will pop into your mind.

With just a little bit of practice, this method has the potential to work miracles in your life that initially are hard to believe. Once you master the technique (and it's not hard to do), it can become a regular problem-solving tool for you to use any time you need it. It is really that powerful, and it has certainly created countless miracles in my life.

The other method I employ is even simpler: I start paying attention to everything around me. I look at businesses while I drive, I listen carefully to everything people say around me, I start listening intently to the lyrics of songs I listen to, and I pay attention to everything else that comes into my sphere of consciousness. I never expect the answer to suddenly show up on a sign or anywhere else, but what often happens is that something I see or hear suddenly creates a connection and sparks an idea.

It's like I'm brainstorming with the world. In a brainstorming session you don't expect someone to come up with the exact answer you seek, although sometimes that does happen. Instead, you're looking for something someone says, something that is often totally unrelated, to spark the connection that makes the answer you seek pop into your mind.

An example of this is when I write a book and need a couple more chapters to fulfill my goal of a certain word count. As described, I start paying attention to everything around me, and on more than one occasion, a lyric in a song I'm listening to in my car suddenly sparks the idea I am looking for. In fact, I've even heard lyrics that became the title of the missing chapter I was seeking.

Another element that affects my creativity — and this does not just mean overcoming writer's block — is where I write. I always look for an inspirational setting, and this influences my choice of homes, where I place my desk, and especially the vacations I take. I almost always write when I am on vacation. I am writing this book while I am in Fiji, although that's not the reason I came here. I am currently in Fiji because I was invited to teach entrepreneurism here to the local population to help boost their economy, an incredible honor for me. Nonetheless, writing while I am here makes my trip even more fulfilling.

I wrote my last book at my vacation home in the Austrian Alps. My house there has a view of mountains, forests, and a gorgeous lake.

Much of my writing is done at my current home in California. I have a desk where I love to spend time. My chair is more like a throne than a chair, a reproduction of Lord Raffles' desk and chair (purchased from Design Toscano).

I cannot tell you precisely how much the location and setting where I write influences my writing, but since they definitely add to my enjoyment, I have to assume that they are worth considering as a contributing factor.

Like everything else in this manual, I am sharing techniques that work for me. There is no set rigid way for doing anything when it comes to writing. Just try the techniques I employ and see which work best for you. Most of them should yield great results for you.

Your Instant Insights...

- Everyone experiences writer's block at some point. The first way to overcome it is to use the method described to get your subconscious mind to come up with new ideas.

- The second method to get new ideas is to pay attention to everything around you, even song lyrics. Something you see or hear may create a connection in your mind and spark the idea that you seek.

- The setting where you write may also impact your creativity. Write in inspirational surroundings.

Marketing – treat it like a business!

It has been said — and it is true, as I will explain in a bit — that the least effective way to make money off a book is by selling the book itself. In addition, many writers also experience a bit of a letdown after their book is published, an anticlimax that I will describe to you shortly also. But the good news is that the process of writing and publishing involves several milestones that are exhilarating and satisfying.

The activity of writing itself can be an incredibly enjoyable activity. Having people read what you wrote and getting positive reviews nourishes your soul in ways you have to experience to fully understand. Seeing your book's cover design for the first time — and loving it — is another great milestone. And of course, at the moment your work is released to the world, making you a published author, you've accomplished an amazing achievement you should be very proud of.

The anticlimax I mentioned often happens when your book is completed and published. Then comes the big question, "Now what?" Assuming you publish your book on Amazon in a downloadable as well as printed format, and assuming you do a weeklong intense marketing campaign to give your book best-seller status in its category, when that campaign is over, you may suddenly feel a slump, no matter how well your campaign went. Your best-seller campaign is over and nothing further seems to be happening. This is not unusual.

At this point in time, marketing has to become your new profession. You see, authors typically don't make much money if they just sit around waiting for their books to sell. The book has to be marketed. YOU have to be marketed. Published authors live in a new world where effective marketing means going in new and creative directions. Book publishing is not what it used to be twenty years ago.

What follows is the single-most effective way to make big money as an author. Here's what you need to know:

As mentioned, your book by itself will not make you much money. But in today's world, your book has value beyond just what you get from its sales. Your book becomes your new business card, establishing you as an expert or authority in your field. Many people still view authors almost like celebrities, despite the fact that getting a book out there is so much easier today because of the advent of self-publishing.

Thus, putting authors on a pedestal because they have accomplished what few people will even attempt to do gives them the leverage to venture into arenas that can make serious money — dramatically more than just selling their book. The main source of that income is in public speaking.

Authors can use their newfound status as an authority in their field to get speaking engagements that can eventually command fees amounting to many thousands of dollars for each time they speak. Imagine how many books you'd have to sell to make that kind of money. This can then move into coaching and consulting, which can also command very attractive incomes.

Speaking engagements can come from businesses, clubs, and seminars. There are even plenty of professionals out there who specialize in getting you booked on stage as often as you can handle it.

The money is there for authors to tap into, but it rarely comes just from book sales. Nonetheless, speaking engagements will have the additional benefit of contributing to increased book sales, which often take place in the back of the room where one is holding a lecture.

The art of public speaking is not the topic of this manual, so you should learn the art from someone who is an accomplished speaker or from a good instructional book. Fortunately, anyone can learn to be a compelling speaker; it is not that hard to learn.

I know that many of you are thinking that being on stage is frightening. For some it is a terrifying thought. But know that anyone can learn to overcome stage fright, so don't shy away from the thought of standing on stage. Like anything else, it is a learnable skill, and once you learn it, it is one of the most enjoyable activities imaginable. Trust me on this. I've been on stage throughout my entire life, and nothing feels quite like the satisfaction you get when your audience is hanging on to your every word.

The point is that your job is not done once your book is published. Now you have to market your book, whether you do it all by yourself or with the help of experts. And marketing and self-promotion is a never-ending process. If you stop marketing, then your income will decline. Find your marketing niche and learn to speak to an audience that is eager to hear the knowledge you have to offer, and you can become rich from it. There are plenty of books out there that can teach you what you need to know.

Like public speaking, marketing is also a learnable skill, one you should either study yourself or hire someone who is already an expert. The exception is if your book is traditionally published, such as with Simon & Schuster, Penguin Random House, etc. But traditional publishers are incredibly picky as to whose book they will publish, and in a sense, it is also a declining industry. Self-publishing, on the other hand, is exploding, but frequently this means just design, editing, and printing — not much else. I believe the future lies with self-publishers who also participate in the marketing of your book, such as my publisher, Crescendo Publishing, who has coordinated the marketing of my books on Amazon to make every one a best seller in its category.

In summary, understand that the release of your book is not the end of the road. Know that there may be a bit of an anticlimactic feeling once you stop marketing and therefore selling your book. Investigate the many roads you can take to give your book visibility, especially the most profitable of them all, public speaking. In today's world, your book will become your new business card. Use it as such and always have some copies handy in the trunk of your car. You never know when giving one to the right person can launch you to higher levels of stardom.

Finally, also consider turning your book into an audio version, as many people prefer to listen to these in their car. On top of that, you can create additional materials, such as workbooks to support your book. Once you have a customer who loves your book, you can upsell them to other products and events.

To do this, you must be able to connect with your readers, most effectively through social media and by collecting e-mail addresses. Your book should therefore have a page with your contact information, including your Facebook, LinkedIn, and Twitter addresses, your e-mail address, and your author website address. On your website, you can give away a free bonus chapter or other gift in return for your prospect's e-mail address. A sizeable e-mail list can be monetized in numerous ways and will become one of your most valuable assets.

The bottom line? Becoming an author is a business like any other and should be treated as such. As the saying goes, "If you want to be a big business tomorrow then you have to start acting like one today."

Your Instant Insights...

- Selling your book is the least effective way to make money as an author. Rather, your book should become your new business card, establishing you as an authority in your field and getting you teaching, speaking, and coaching engagements.

- Marketing yourself and your new book should become your new business, and you should treat it like a business.

- Public speaking is an immensely enjoyable skill anyone can learn, even those who are afraid of being on stage.

The joy of writing!

In all the books I have written, there is a common ingredient I always bring up because of its supreme importance: To be as good as you possibly can be at something, you have to enjoy it. If it becomes a genuine passion, then you have the potential to become a superstar in that field. This applies to writing just as it does to any other endeavor — business or otherwise. If you don't enjoy the act of writing, then it will always remain a struggle for you, and the quality of your work will suffer. There are several reasons for this.

First, if you enjoy something, then you have the energy and motivation to get up in the morning to do it. If you love something, then it's not work. However, if you don't enjoy the process, then it becomes a drag, leading to endless reasons to procrastinate and to sluggish effort.

Loving what you do also keeps you from quitting. After all, you're doing it because you love doing it.

And what is it that you want to do the most? That which you love doing, of course.

As a writer, being passionate about writing is the most powerful force that will help you overcome all hurdles, such as writer's block, lack of knowledge in some areas, and of course, giving up when those obstacles appear (as they inevitably will at some point). No matter what the obstacle, if you love writing, then you won't give up ... because you love writing!

Finally, enjoying the process of writing will enable you to learn whatever it is you need to learn about your topic and about the skills required for writing. You'll be able to learn it in no time.

Have you ever read something you weren't interested in? You end up reading it over and over again, but it still won't sink in. Read something you're passionate about and you'll remember every word; you won't be able to get enough of it.

Writing is an immensely satisfying process for me for several reasons, and you may explore how to create the same joys within yourself as I explain them to you.

Writing is an act of creation for me. I love to create something out of nothing. I love to invent things or bring a new method of perception to a topic. The final outcome is an accomplishment that nourishes my soul.

The process of writing and then reviewing what I wrote over and over again, making little adjustments as I go along, for me is like a flower blossoming. With every review, that flower gets more beautiful as I improve on my words, the flow, the tone, the sequence, until I finally manage to say what I want to say in a way that people can easily understand and follow. It is like a sculptor chipping away at a block of marble to create a perfect statue. As the sculptor *sees* when their statue has turned out exactly the way they envisioned it, a writer *feels* when their text gets to where they wanted it. The same goes for me. It is a feeling that tells me when I'm done revising and everything is just right.

An important aspect of my endless proofreading and incremental improvements is the time period between writing and reading. I reread paragraphs and chapters after I complete them, but I also reread them again with at least twenty-four hours having passed since I wrote the text. Different periods of time spent away from your text make you read that text with different eyes. Your perception of the same text is different after you've had time to clear your mind and forget about your text for a while. It allows you to catch things that you would otherwise miss if you didn't spend time away. For me, this practice is critical.

Next, a most satisfying aspect of writing for me is when I have a chapter in my mind and can't wait to sit down to put it on paper. I go into a different world, almost into a mental cocoon, where time stands still and nothing outside my cocoon affects me as I operate in a world of creativity and productivity. Nothing compares. Many people call it "the zone." Once you experience it for the first time, you'll know exactly what I am talking about.

But the most satisfying result that writing brings me is when I see the effect my lessons have on other people. Most of my books are about the skills you need to become successful in any endeavor you choose, without chance of failure. I teach people how to escape their nine-to-five misery and live their life's passion. Nothing fulfills me more than when I see a budding entrepreneur take my lessons to heart and become successful as a result of them.

Many studies have been done regarding what makes people happiest. Giving and helping others are always at the top of the list, which is what my books represent to me, a means of giving back to the world for all the blessings I have had in my life. It is not about making money. I often give away books for free, and I often coach people for free. It is about the process of writing and creating and then seeing the fruits of my labor have a positive impact on the lives of my readers. I simply cannot imagine anything more fulfilling. That's what success means to me: doing something I love, making a good living from it, and thereby getting a sense of fulfillment from what I've done.

Are you going to sit down as a beginner and immediately love the process when your writing may not yet be at a level where the words flow spontaneously from you in an almost poetic sequence? Of course not. But you can learn to love the process as you get better and better at what you do. You can get to the point where you cannot wait to figure out the topic for your next chapter so that you can dive into your mental cocoon as you tune out the material world and put it all on paper. Get to that point and you'll become a prolific author who will never want to stop writing books.

Your Instant Insights...

- Once you learn to enjoy the process of writing, you will become a much better writer — and writing can be an immensely satisfying activity.

- Enjoying the process keeps you motivated and keeps you from quitting. It also enables you to learn everything you need to learn very quickly.

- Many writers talk about going into a different world when they write, "the zone," where the outside world is tuned out and time seems to stand still. They all love going into this mental cocoon.

About the Author

For twenty-five years, Parviz Firouzgar has owned numerous multimillion-dollar companies in a variety of industries, sometimes running several ventures simultaneously, both for-profit and nonprofit entities.

Some of Parviz's companies involved the use of investor funds of up to several million dollars: when Parviz was just in his twenties, one investor walked away with $1.7 million in one year as a result of his confidence in the author's abilities.

Parviz founded a mortgage company and employed over 500 loan officers. He wrote business plans for start-up companies that helped them raise many millions in start-up capital. After he discovered a new way of raising funds, he expanded into the charitable arena. Within one year, his company was supporting 2,300 needy children around the world, providing all their food, clothing, and education.

Parviz has been in the direct mail and sweepstakes businesses, mailing so many pieces of mail each month (millions) that his local post office had to expand their operations. Most recently, he has been in the precious metals and diamond business, including owning a gold mine.

Parviz was a radio talk-show host and a longtime instructor for Income Builders International (IBI), now called CEO Space, an entrepreneurial forum with internationally recognized instructors such as Jack Canfield, Mark Victor Hansen, Bob Proctor, T. Harv Eker, John Gray, and Lisa Nichols.

Most recently, Parviz has been invited to teach entrepreneurism in Fiji by friends and advisors of the Fijian prime minister. They chose Parviz to help stimulate their economy. Parviz does this for free several times per year.

Raised in Europe, Parviz speaks four languages. He has been accepted for membership in Mensa and Intertel, both high-IQ societies.

Connect with the Author

Websites:
www.successlibrary.com

Email:
pfirouzgar@gmail.com

Social Media:
Facebook: www.facebook.com/pfirouzgar

LinkedIn: www.linkedin.com/pub/parviz-firouzgar/
b6/8b4/91

Twitter: @ParvizFirouzgar

Mailing Address:
13681 Newport Ave. #8-619,
Tustin, CA 92780

Other books by Parviz Firouzgar
(all available on Amazon)

Side Effects May Include Happiness
How to trade your 9-to-5 misery for your life's passion!

20/20 Hindsight
If I knew then what I know now I'd be a whole lot richer!

20/20 Hindsight (Part II)
Additional lessons for entrepreneurs you won't learn about in business school!

The Secrets of Wealth
Discover the financial principles responsible for every fortune ever made and learn to use these principles to create your own fortune!

Motivation
Your master key for success & riches!
(another *Instant Insights*™ book)

About Crescendo Publishing

Crescendo Publishing is a boutique-style, concierge VIP publishing company assisting entrepreneurs with writing, publishing, and promoting their books for the purposes of lead-generation and achieving global platform growth, then monetizing it for even more income opportunities.

Check out some of our latest best-selling AuthorPreneurs at
http://CrescendoPublishing.com/new-authors

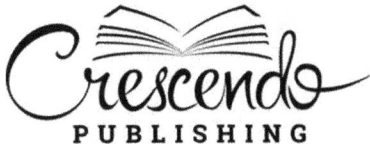

About the Instant Insights™ Book Series

The *Instant Insights™ Book Series* is a fact-only, short-read, book series written by EXPERTS in very specialized categories. These high-value, high-quality books can be produced in ONLY 6-8 weeks, from concept to launch, in BOTH PRINT & eBOOK Formats!

This book series is FOR YOU if:

- You are an expert in your niche or area of specialty

- You want to write a book to position yourself as an expert

- You want YOUR OWN book – NOT a chapter in someone else's book

- You want to have a book to give to people when you're speaking at events or simply networking

- You want to have it available quickly

- You don't have the time to invest in writing a 200-page full book

- You don't have a ton of money to invest in the production of a full book – editing, cover design, interior layout, best-seller promotion

- You don't have a ton of time to invest in finding quality contractors for the production of your book – editing, cover design, interior layout, best-seller promotion

For more information on how you can become an *Instant Insights™* author, visit
www.InstantInsightsBooks.com

More Books in the
Instant Insight™ Series

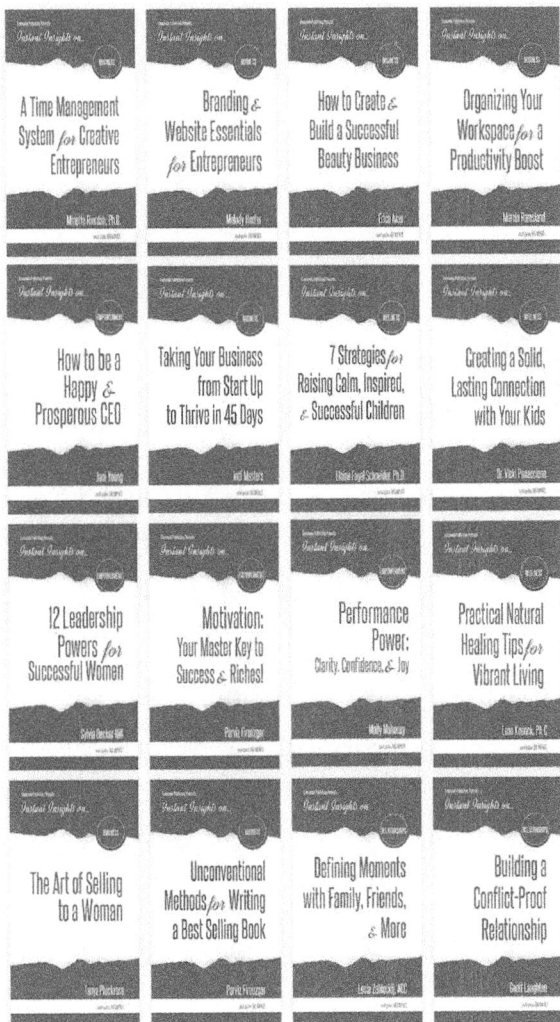

A Time Management System *for* **Creative Entrepreneurs**	**Branding** *&* **Website Essentials** *for* **Entrepreneurs**	**How to Create** *&* **Build a Successful Beauty Business**	**Organizing Your Workspace** *for* **a Productivity Boost**
How to be a Happy *&* **Prosperous CEO**	**Taking Your Business from Start Up to Thrive in 45 Days**	**7 Strategies** *for* **Raising Calm, Inspired,** *&* **Successful Children**	**Creating a Solid, Lasting Connection with Your Kids**
12 Leadership Powers *for* **Successful Women**	**Motivation:** **Your Master Key to Success** *&* **Riches!**	**Performance Power:** Clarity, Confidence, *&* Joy	**Practical Natural Healing Tips** *for* **Vibrant Living**
The Art of Selling to a Woman	**Unconventional Methods** *for* **Writing a Best Selling Book**	**Defining Moments with Family, Friends,** *&* **More**	**Building a Conflict-Proof Relationship**

Crescendo
CrescendoPublishing.com

www.ingramcontent.com/pod-product-compliance
Lightning Source LLC
Chambersburg PA
CBHW071348290326
41933CB00041B/3052